COLONIAL PEOPLE

# The Colonial Wigmaker

LAURA L. SULLIVAN

Cavendish Square

**New York**

Published in 2016 by Cavendish Square Publishing, LLC
243 5th Avenue, Suite 136, New York, NY 10016

Copyright © 2016 by Cavendish Square Publishing, LLC

First Edition

Website: cavendishsq.com

This publication represents the opinions and views of the author based on his or her personal experience, knowledge, and research. The information in this book serves as a general guide only. The author and publisher have used their best efforts in preparing this book and disclaim liability rising directly or indirectly from the use and application of this book.

CPSIA Compliance Information: Batch #WS15CSQ

All websites were available and accurate when this book was sent to press.

Library of Congress Cataloging-in-Publication Data

Sullivan, Laura L., 1974-
The colonial wigmaker / Laura L. Sullivan.
pages cm. — (Colonial people)
Includes bibliographical references and index.
ISBN 978-1-50260-480-4 (hardcover) ISBN 978-1-50260-481-1 (ebook)
1. Wigs—United States—History—18th century—Juvenile literature.
2. Wigmakers—United States—History—18th century—Juvenile literature.
3. United States—Social life and customs—To 1775—Juvenile literature. I. Title.

TT975.S85 2016
679.0973—dc23

2014049220

Editorial Director: David McNamara
Editor: Andrew Coddington
Copy Editor: Cynthia Roby
Art Director: Jeffrey Talbot
Designer: Stephanie Flecha
Senior Production Manager: Jennifer Ryder-Talbot
Production Editor: Renni Johnson
Photo Research: J8 Media

The photographs in this book are used by permission and through the courtesy of: Lake County Museum/Getty Images, cover; North Wind Picture Archives, 4; File:Matronalivia2.jpg/Wikimedia Commons, 6; Public Domain/http://www.marileecody.com/gloriana/elizabethrainbow1.jpg/ File:Elizabeth I Rainbow Portrait.jpg/Wikipedia/Wikimedia Commons, 8; Public Domain/File:Ex-voto a sainte-genevieve -Detail-Largilliere. jpg/Wikimedia Commons, 11; Stock Montage/Archive Photos/Getty Images, 12; Wellcome Images/Wellcome Trust, United Kingdom/File:Barber-surgeons operating on a boil on a man's forehead. Oil Wellcome V0017569.jpg/Wikimedia Commons, 14; Hulton Archive/Getty Images, 19; Wellcome Images (http://wellcomeimages.org/), a website operated by Wellcome Trust, a global charitable foundation based in the United Kingdom/ File:Perriquier Barbier by R. Benard after Lucotte Wellcome L0005156.jpg/Wikimedia Commons, 21; Colonial Williamsburg Foundation, 23, 25, 29, 33; Wellcome Library, London/Hair and wigdressing equipment. Engraving by R. Bénard after J.R. Lucotte, 1762, 26; Archives Charmet/Bridgeman Images, 31; Visions of America/UIG/Getty Images, 37; Library of Congress/File:Writing the Declaration of Independence 1776 cph.3g09904.jpg/ Wikimedia Commons, 38; Gareth Cattermole/Getty Images, 42.

Printed in the United States of America

# CONTENTS

# ONE

## Wigs Throughout History

Humans around the world have an obsession with hair. Although our ancestors lost their pelts about three million years ago, we kept the hair on our heads. There is some variation among people living in different parts of the world, but most people—at least for part of their lives—can grow long, thick locks. And nearly every culture has been interested in styling, decorating, and preserving their hair.

Some scientists think hair remained on the head for temperature regulation or to protect the head from the sun's rays. Others think it has a social function, or to help in mate selection. It could be that healthy hair was a sign of overall health. Someone with good hair could be considered a potential husband or wife. Or hair could simply be an ornament to attract people, like a peacock tail or a mandrill's blue face.

*English citizens, such as these conferring with King Charles II, received charters to start new colonies in the Americas.*

Whatever the reason for head hair, throughout history there have been people who wanted more hair, or different hair. What they couldn't grow, they made or bought. People in many historical eras have worn **wigs**—false arrangements of real or artificial hair—to supplement or replace their own locks.

## Wigs in Egypt

As long as five thousand years ago, Egyptians were making wigs out of everything from human hair to wool to fibers from the leaves of

palm trees. Both men and women wore wigs in ancient Egypt, though men's wigs were often fancier. Most people shaved their heads, and wore wigs for reasons of either fashion or ceremony.

Egyptian wigs weren't meant to fool anyone. Even when they were made of human hair they were usually coated with beeswax to look stiff and unnatural. Some

*Roman women, such as this one from around 80–90 CE, could achieve elaborate hairstyles with the use of wigs and artificial hairpieces.*

were even made of silver. Others were dyed with **henna**, which would make dark hair auburn, and light or gray hair vibrant orange. At parties, women would sometimes wear cones of perfume in their hair, which would melt in the Egyptian heat as the night progressed.

## Greek and Roman Wigs

Greeks and Romans used wigs too. Greeks were embarrassed by baldness because slaves' heads were shaved, so Greek men would wear wigs to hide their bare heads. Early Romans didn't often wear wigs, but by the time of the Roman Empire (beginning in 31 BCE) wigs became a popular fashion statement. Hair was taken from slaves and women captured in the places Romans invaded. Light-colored hair from people in what is present-day France and Germany was widely used.

## Medieval and Renaissance Wigs

Around the Middle Ages, women were encouraged to cover their heads, so ornamentation wasn't possible. Everyone was expected to dress plainly, without much decoration. The church forbade the wearing of wigs. By the sixteenth century, though, **aristocratic** women were wearing wigs as fashion statements. Queen Elizabeth I of England had at least eighty wigs.

In the seventeenth century, the French kings Louis XIII and Louis XIV set the trend when they wore elaborate wigs to hide their thinning hair (or possibly for medical reasons). All of their courtiers followed their lead. The fashion spread to England.

## The Rise of the English Wig

The English fashion for wigs was temporarily interrupted by the English Civil War (1642–1651) when Parliamentarians fought Royalists and executed King Charles I. The puritanical Parliamentarians were also known as Roundheads, because they shunned long hair and wigs, instead keeping their hair short or shaved.

When Charles II reclaimed the throne in 1660, wigs were once again standard, particularly

*Queen Elizabeth I (1533–1603) had many wigs made to match her naturally red hair.*

for men. Many wore elaborate wigs with huge curls and ringlets. Though in 1665 the famous diarist Samuel Pepys wrote that he was afraid to buy a wig, fearing the hair might have been cut from someone who died of the plague, or Black Death, still they remained fashionable.

## Puritans Protest Periwigs

When English settlers came to North America in the early 1600s to establish the colonies, they carried many of the Old World traditions with them. Though wigs and fashion weren't a top priority for the earliest generations—as they focused on survival—later colonists were just as sophisticated as the people in Europe.

Many of the early settlers in the New England colonies were **Puritans**. This pious group of Protestants was against most forms of pleasure, diversion, and ornamentation. They preferred instead to focus on strict religious rules. Some Puritan ministers condemned people who wore wigs. Others, though, called it an innocent fashion, and thought it should be allowed.

The puritan minister and Harvard president Increase Mather called wigs "horrid bushes of vanity." However, his son Cotton Mather, also a minister, always wore wigs, as did several other clergy members. Soon all of the undergraduates at Harvard were wearing wigs, setting the style in the colonies.

# Health, Medicine, and Wigs

Lush, healthy hair is often seen as a sign of overall health. But some diseases can cause hair to thin, and even fall out. One disease called syphilis ran rampant in the sixteenth and seventeenth centuries. Among the many unpleasant symptoms—including, ultimately, madness and death—was hair loss. The disease itself caused hair to fall out and so did its cure: people ingested potions containing toxic mercury and arsenic to fight syphilis.

*Men who wore wigs and face patches might have been covering up a deadly (and contagious) disease like syphilis.*

Some historians think that that the rise of wig use in this time, particularly for fashionable, wealthy young men, was to hide the fact that they had syphilis. Other fashion trends might have been related to illness, too. Syphilis could cause skin lesions. Smallpox, another common disease of the era, caused sores and often left deep pits on the skin. Hair (wigs or natural) was worn in big curls around the forehead and cheeks, perhaps to hide sores. Gloves also became common to cover more affected skin. Many fashionable women and even men wore decorative black patches glued to their face to hide pimples, sores, and scars.

## Wigs in the Southern Colonies

Wigs were common in the southern colonies from the earliest days of settlement. Everyone wanted to show his or her wealth and status by wearing a wig. Wealthy plantation owners had many wigs, while even laborers often had one. While these might have been of poor quality compared to those owned by the wealthy, it was a status symbol everyone hoped to have if he wished to appear properly dressed. Male slaves who worked indoors were usually given a wig, and

slaves who worked outdoors sometimes made their own wigs out of cotton or animal hair.

Eventually, wigs became the standard for gentlemen throughout the colonies. A man of wealth and status was not considered to be properly dressed unless he was wearing a wig. As the decades progressed, wigs became (for the most part) smaller and less ornate. But their popularity continued until after the American Revolutionary War.

*Colonial New England Puritan minister Cotton Mather defied his father and other clergy members by wearing a wig.*

# TWO

## Becoming a Wigmaker

Before there were wigmakers, there were **barbers**. The word barber comes from the Latin word for beard. Today, a barber is more likely to cut hair than to shave a beard. But for many centuries shaving was a tricky and dangerous business, done with deadly sharp straight razors. Most men relied on a professional to shave them. A barber could always keep his blades sharp, give a close shave, and take care around a man's vulnerable throat and face.

### The Barber-Surgeon

Since they were known to have the sharpest blades, early barbers often practiced medical trades, too. The **barber-surgeon** would perform

*Early barbers took advantage of their supply of sharp blades to shave clients and perform minor surgeries such as bloodletting.*

surgical procedures and dentistry. (There were trained physicians at the time, but they usually preferred not to touch patients. They mostly observed patients and prescribed remedies.)

People believed that bloodletting could cure some ailments, so the barber would deftly slice open a small vein and drain out a pint or two of blood. He might also keep leeches to take smaller amounts of blood. The barber would usually just perform minor procedures, such as lancing a boil or pulling a tooth. (**Blacksmiths** also pulled teeth, because they were strong and had pliers handy.) But barber-surgeons might also be called on to do serious surgery, such as an amputation.

## More Profit in Wigs

In 1540, barber-surgeons had their own guild, or association of tradesmen. But by the seventeenth century surgery was becoming a specialized profession. Barbers weren't allowed to operate on people anymore. They needed a new way to make money besides just shaving beards and trimming hair.

When the wig craze started in France, England, and later in the North American colonies, barbers saw an opportunity for **profit**. A well-made wig was extremely expensive. By the late colonial period, every man wanted to have one—though not everyone could afford a good wig.

It is estimated that only about 5 percent of the population could afford a custom-made wig. (Many people have the impression that every man in colonial America wore a wig, because today we only see the colonists through surviving portraits. These paintings are almost always of wealthy people, who could better afford a wig than laborers or the poor.) A wig might cost the equivalent of several weeks' wages. A yearly contract for shaving and wig maintenance was about £2 ($3.15 USD) in the 1700s. (By comparison, a sailor with the East India Company might make less than £2, or $3.15 USD, a month, while a schoolteacher might make about £5, or $7.87 USD, per month.)

Wigs were status symbols. They showed that a man had money to spend, and lots of leisure time to attend to his wig. Barbers seized the chance to make more money. Most decided to be wigmakers first, and barbers second. They still shaved their customers, but their primary purpose was to make and care for wigs.

## The Apprentice Wigmaker

In much of Europe from the Middle Ages onward, craftsmen organized in guilds, meaning associations that control who can practice a particular art or trade. To join the guild, a young man or woman had to go through a system of training. First, they were **apprentices**, then **journeymen**. Finally, if they were capable of producing a masterpiece in their field, they were considered **master** craftsmen and admitted to their guild.

By the time English colonists arrived in North America, the guild system was falling out of favor. Still, most people learned trades by being apprenticed to a master. Wig making was no exception. At first, most of the best wigmakers came directly from London, but wigmakers began training in the colonies as time went on.

A skilled wigmaker would take on an apprentice, meaning a young person who was bound to the master to learn his trade for a fixed period. Most apprenticeships lasted seven years, but they range from five to nine years. Often they were timed to end when the apprentice turned twenty-one. The child's parents would usually pay the wigmaker a sum of money to train the apprentice. The apprentice often lived with the master wigmaker, and had to follow his rules. An apprentice wasn't generally paid for his work, but he might receive a set of clothes or wig-making tools when his contract was over.

## The Master Wigmaker

When the apprentice wigmaker had finished training, he became a journeyman. A journeyman could receive payment for his work. He might continue working for his previous master, or he might work for someone else. If he had enough money, he could set up a shop for himself. People didn't always use the titles of journeyman and

# Wig Words

The original word for a wig was *peruke*, which was used in France beginning in the fifteenth century. The English adopted this word, but changed it to *perwyck*. Later, the English corrupted it to periwig. The word wig is an abbreviation of periwig.

The richer and more important the seventeenth- and early eighteenth-century man was, the larger his wig. The term bigwig is still used today to refer to an important or powerful person.

Sometimes, a thief would yank a person's wig over their face to distract them while

*Wealthy people and wigmakers often had a separate room strictly for powdering their wigs because the process created a mess.*

they were being robbed. (Or he'd be stealing the valuable wig itself.) And some young men would pull people's wigs over their eyes to tease them. Wigs were white like wool, and sometimes actually made from animal hair. So the phrase "pull the wool over one's eyes" has come to mean fooling or deceiving someone.

A person had to maintain good posture, or his wig would fall off. Some people think this is the origin of the phrase "flip your wig," meaning to lose your composure or go crazy. The term "wig out" means the same thing.

Nowadays, a lady might excuse herself to the powder room when she wants to be coy about going to the bathroom. In colonial times, the powder room wasn't a toilet, but rather a place where gentlemen could have their wigs powdered—a messy process.

master, though. The only difference was whether the wigmaker kept his own shop or worked for someone else.

Though most wigmakers were men, women could also be apprenticed and learn the trade. Or, they might learn to make wigs because their father was a wigmaker. Poor **widows** were sometimes encouraged to learn wig making. The trade would provide them, and their families, an income.

# THREE

## A Visit to the Wigmaker

When a gentleman was in the market for a new wig, the wigmaker offered him a dazzling array of choices. Nearly all wigs were custom made, and the buyer could choose his favorite color and style.

Wigs were available in a variety of colors. Earlier in the colonial period (before the eighteenth century) people wore wigs in black, brown, blonde, auburn, white, or gray. Another popular hue was a mixture of both white and black or gray hair, which was called **grizzle**. A strong red color was available but unpopular.

Later, the prevailing style was for light-colored or white wigs. At first wigmakers tried bleaching darker hair to lighten it. Unfortunately, the bleaching weakened the hair and made it unsuitable for wig making. Later, the desired color was achieved mostly with powder made from a mix of flour, white clay, starch, and plaster of Paris. The

*A thriving wigmaker's shop might have several employees. Each was always busy shaving or measuring customers, and making or styling wigs.*

powder was most commonly white or off-white, but a particularly fashion-conscious man might wear light purple, blue, or pink powder. The powder was often blended with a pleasing scent, such as lavender or orange flower.

## What Kind of Hair?

Next, the customer had to decide what kind of hair he wanted. Human hair was the best, and most expensive, choice. Women who needed money could sell their long hair. The hair was usually imported from Europe.

Less expensive wigs might be made with animal hair. Fur from the yak, a long-haired cowlike animal from the Himalayan Mountains and Tibet, was considered the best animal hair. Next was goat fur, and then hair from a horse's mane and tail. A wig might also be made from wool. Sometimes goat or yak hair was used for "baby hair"—the little wisps at the hairline that were supposed to make the wig look more natural. (On the other hand, some people were said to deliberately let their real hairline show, so everyone would know they were wearing a wig, not their own hair.)

## Choosing a Style

A wigmaker could offer his customer one of more than a hundred different styles of wig. In the 1600s, wigs tended to be very big, featuring elaborate, flowing curls. They sometimes had huge puffs of frizz. During the 1700s, wigs were usually smaller, but often more detailed. They would have different arrangements of waves, curls, and braids, depending on the customer's taste and the fashion of the time. A wealthy man might have a different wig for every occasion: riding, business, evening parties, and casual daytime wear. Certain professions even had their preferred wig styles.

## Wigs for Soldiers and Dandies

Soldiers often wore a style called the *Ramillies* wig. This wig usually had three small curls on each side of the face, stacked one on top of

*There were dozens of different styles of wig to choose from in colonial America.*

the other (not side-by-side ringlets). Long hair would hang down the back in a tight braid or queue, with a big bow at the top of the braid, and a little bow at the bottom. Soldiers who couldn't afford a wig often wore their natural hair in this style. George Washington refused to wear a wig, but styled his own hair in the Ramillies fashion.

Travelers and some people in the military wore a campaign wig, a wavy wig about eighteen inches long, with a small twisted lock on each side. A bagwig had curls at the front and sides, and very long hair in the back. The hair was tucked inside a decorative, square silk bag.

## Major and Minor Bobs

One of the most popular wig styles was the Sunday buckle, also called the "major bob." This was a conservative, helmet-shaped wig consisting of several rows of stacked curls close to the head, without any tail or flowing locks.

Apprentices, and other people of low station who still aspired to fashion, often wore the minor bob. This wig was very bushy, parted down the center, with a small tail or queue at the back. Because it was mostly loose, without any small curls, that kind of wig required little styling or upkeep.

## Shave and Measure

Once the customer selected all the details of his wig, the wigmaker would shave his head. He might also shave his facial hair at the same time. The wigmaker (or more likely his apprentice or journeyman) would drape the customer in a cloth to protect his clothes, apply a soapy lather with a boar-bristle brush, and shave his head and face with a sharp straight razor. Without any hair in the way, he could make sure the wig had a perfect, snug fit.

The wigmaker would use strips of paper to measure different angles of his customer's head—side to side, front to back, over the top, and even from the center of the forehead to each temple. After that,

*In addition to shaving a customer's head, a wigmaker might also shave a customer's face before a fitting.*

the customer could go home, returning only to try on the finished wig and pay for it. (He would have worn an old wig or else a turban or velvet cap on the way home.)

## Tempering Hair

Human hair had to be treated before it was ready for use. First, it was doused in flour and sand. This would soak up any oils remaining

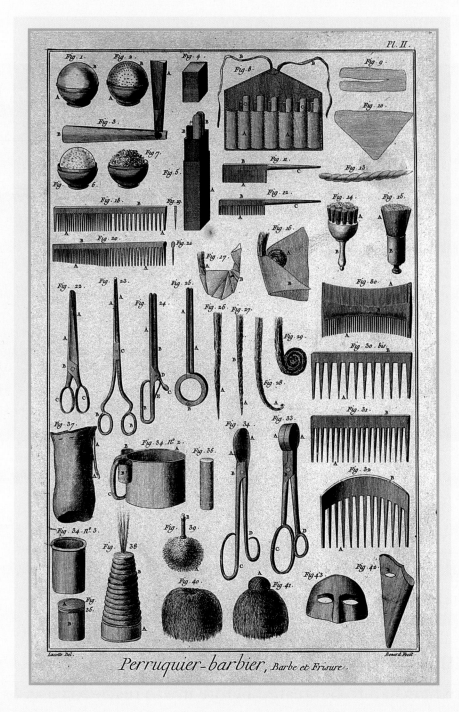

A wigmaker used many tools, including combs, hackles, and curling irons.

on the hair. Next, the hair was pulled through a metal-toothed comb called a hackle. This removed any tangles and made the hair smooth. It was then separated into small parcels.

Then it was subject to a variety of treatments for **tempering**. This made the hair stronger so the wig would last a long time and withstand the curling, brushing, and styling to which it would be subjected. Generally the hair was wound around a curling rod made of clay. It was then boiled for several hours, and dried in a small oven.

For hair that was to be used in a particularly frizzy style, an additional technique was used. A bundle of boiled and dried parcels of hair would be put into cheesecloth and then sent to the local baker or gingerbread maker. He would cover the bunch of hair parcels with a paste of rye flour, and then bake them in his big oven. When the rye loaf was cracked open, the hair inside would be set in the desired frizz.

## Assembling the Wig

Finally, the wigmaker could begin to assemble the wig. He made a pattern, which showed him how many rows of hair he needed, the size of each row, as well as the length of hair needed for each particular part of the wig. He used a weaving frame to attach hair (root-end first) to silk threads to make a weft. Several strands of hair were attached at one time. Many strips of weft were needed for each wig. Attaching all of the hair needed for a wig took many hours.

Next, the wigmaker created a **caul**—a cap that would fit closely on the customer's head. Often a customer would have a wooden likeness of his own head carved exactly to his measurements. It could be used when making the caul and wig, or for storing the wig. This was called a wig block, from which we get the term "blockhead" or stupid person.

The first layer of the caul was made of strips of silk ribbon, sewn into the shape of a head. Over this, the wigmaker attached netting, and then two strips of wide covering ribbon. He usually added a drawstring or buckle at the back, so the customer could tighten the wig.

Starting at the back, the wigmaker would sew the strips of hair into place. When all of the hair was attached to the caul, the wigmaker was ready to finish the wig. This process involved trimming, styling, and locking the style into place.

## Finishing a Wig

The colonists didn't have hairspray and gel, but they had other ways to keep their style in position. Hair was first smeared with **pomatum**, a type of ointment made from animal fat such as hog lard or bear grease and mixed with beeswax and scented oils such

as clove or thyme. It was then curled around hot tongs or rolled in papers. Then more pomatum was painted onto the arrangement, and it was thoroughly powdered. When the mixture dried, it was quite hard, and kept the wig arrangement in place. The wig might then be spritzed with perfume. Now it was ready for its new owner.

## Wig Maintenance

Making and setting the wig was just the first step. Wigs needed considerable maintenance. They had to be washed periodically, and reset. Many customers bought a yearly contract so they could be shaved and have their wig touched up once every two weeks.

*A wig required frequent maintenance. The wigmaker would often wash and restyle his customers' wigs.*

# Women's Hair

As a rule, colonial women did not wear wigs. Most arranged their own hair or had a servant do it for them. It was usually worn up and back, away from the face, with a few ringlets hanging down the back or over the shoulder. Older women, and those from more conservative areas, wore simpler styles or covered their hair. Women might add decorative combs, pins, or arrangements of dried flowers.

Some, though, copied the more exaggerated styles of Europe. Aristocratic women in France wore some of the

Cœffure à l'Independance ou le Triomphe de la liberté

*Aristocratic French women sometimes wore ridiculously big wigs and hairpieces, such as this one with an entire model ship. Few colonial American women followed these styles, but some came close.*

largest, most elaborate hairdos the world has ever seen. But most of the time, they didn't wear actual wigs. They supplemented their own hair with false hairpieces—large twists and clusters of ringlets. They also used forms to wrap their own hair around, giving it support for sometimes-massive structures. Whether through use of wigs or hairpieces, they could make their hair 3 feet (0.9 meters) high. It might even be a themed hairdo, with all of the signs of the zodiac, or even a model ship sailing on their waves, complete with tiny firing cannons.

Few colonists went that far, but they might supplement their own hair with a few false curls. Wigmakers were happy to oblige the ladies with these smaller pieces.

Some wigmakers offered house calls. They would come to the customer's home and arrange the wig in private. Other customers sent their wig to the wigmaker for service. They might not be thoroughly washed and reset, but they would still be smoothed, primped, and scented to be fresh. It was common to see apprentice wigmakers dashing through the streets on a Saturday afternoon, delivering cleaned and set wigs for that night's parties.

# FOUR

## The Wigmaker in the Community

Most people wore simple clothes, tied their own hair in an easy style, and worked hard just to survive. But among the elite of the colonies, there was a keen interest in fashion and a desire to show off taste and wealth. Wigs were only part of the fashion at the time. There was a thriving dressmaking and tailoring business in the colonies, which complemented the wig-making business.

### Men's Fashion

A man of fashion would coordinate his wig with his clothes. Light-colored or white wigs were considered best for evening wear, because they reflected the light better than dark wigs. The typical outfit for the fashionable man was the coat, waistcoat (or vest), and breeches—pants that came to the knee or slightly below. To this he would add hose

*Wealthy colonial men and women showed off their status through fine clothes, wigs, and accessories.*

and buckled shoes, and a cravat, or neck cloth. Even when some wig styles made it impossible for a man to wear a hat, he was usually expected to carry it under his arm.

## Women's Fashion

A well-dressed woman would usually wear a gown, consisting of a bodice (the top part of a dress) attached to the skirt. The front of the skirt would be open, revealing a petticoat that was not an undergarment but was supposed to be seen. They often wore a frame or hoop under their skirt to give it greater volume. Indoors, a woman would wear a linen, cotton, or lace cap. When she went outside she would tie a broad brimmed hat over the cap. Women wore stays, or laced undergarments around their torsos.

## The Shipping Trade

Much of the hair for wigs, as well as the silk thread and ribbon used to create them, was imported. The shipping industry was vital for the wig trade. Other important parts of fashion were also imported. Many of the best fabrics, such as silk or fine woolen broadcloth, came from overseas, even if the final garment was made locally.

Accessories for wigs, and for fashion in general, usually weren't made domestically. Jewels for women, watches for men, and ivory or tortoiseshell combs for hair and wigs were all shipped in from overseas.

## The Woodworkers

Wigmakers relied on woodworkers to create the wig blocks they used to design, style, and store the wigs they made. Sometimes a woodcarver or furniture maker would make wig blocks as a sideline, but occasionally someone would specialize in making woodenheads. He was called a blocker, or blockhead carver.

A wigmaker would have several sizes of woodenheads in his shop. He tried to get as close as possible to the range of head sizes of his customers. A more successful wigmaker would have a greater variety of blocks. Most people who owned a wig also had one—or several—of these blocks to hold and store their wigs when they weren't in use. A custom-carved blockhead could capture the owner's exact dimensions. Some fancy wig blocks even had doors in the back or side, perfect for storing hair combs or pins.

## The Community

Everyone in colonial America was part of a community, and the wigmaker was no exception. A laundress collected the cloths a wigmaker used to protect his customers while he shaved them, and returned the towels clean and fresh. The miller ground up flour that would become part of the white wig powder. An apothecary or herbalist might supply the scented oils a wigmaker used in his pomatum. A pewtersmith would make the scissors used to trim the hair, and a traveling tinker or knife sharpener would hone their edges.

## A Home for Gossip

The wigmaker might play a political role, too. Even today, the barbershop is a place where people can relax and gossip. The colonial wigmaker's shop, where the wigmaker served as barber and wig designer, was much the same. When colonists were becoming uneasy with British rule, they might have aired their grievances to their wigmaker. He could then keep their secrets—or help spread rebellion against the British by repeating tales of dissatisfaction and resistance.

The wigmaker was even involved in what the colonists saw as unfair British taxation. In September 1730, the Assembly of New York decreed that a tax of three shillings should be levied against

# Lice and Stench

Colonial people almost never took a full bath. Without plumbing, it might take a servant as many as sixty trips from a well or other water source to fill a tub. Most people washed their hands and face every day, and perhaps sponged the rest of their body once or twice a week. With no deodorant and minimal hygiene, everyone smelled pretty ripe. But no one noticed as long as they all smelled that way.

With little bathing, people were prone to getting lice. These could live on the body, but were especially fond of the hair. Wigs were one way to combat lice. It is very hard to rid hair (especially long hair) of lice, but a wig could simply be boiled, killing all the vermin. Wig wearers shaved their real hair, so it was easy to pick out any surviving lice.

But wig wearers also received other uninvited guests. Pomatums made of pig fat and suet would attract flies and other insects. Powders infused with floral scents might attract bees. Fortunately, some of the other oils added to wig pomatum, such as thyme and clove oils, are natural insect repellants.

any person who wore or owned a wig made of human, horse, or other kind of hair. The money was to be used to pay British soldiers who were in New York. Many colonists disagreed with this British tax.

## The Military

The wigmaker had a close relationship with the military. Officers were usually expected to wear wigs. Early in the period they wore the elaborate styles that were more suited to a royal court than the battlefield. Later, they adopted a simpler style, usually with a few curls at the temples and a long braid or queue down the back.

Regular soldiers usually could not afford wigs, yet they were expected to wear their hair in a similar style. Most would slick their hair back with tallow or some other kind of animal grease, and braid their hair into a tight queue. Some would still visit the wigmaker for a false queue, and attach the braid to their own hair with a bow.

*Officers in both the British army and the colonial militia usually either wore wigs or arranged their hair to mimic popular wig styles.*

# FIVE

## The Wigmaker's Legacy

Most people couldn't afford a wig, and even the wealthiest members of society sometimes shunned them. While Thomas Jefferson had many wigs, George Washington refused to wear one. Inventor and statesman Benjamin Franklin hated wigs. When visiting France, he wore a fur hat instead. His friends finally persuaded him to have a wig made when he was to meet the king of France. But at the last minute he flung it off and met the king bareheaded. No one objected—they liked his easy, accessible, American style.

The Revolutionary War (1775–1783) sounded the death knell for the wig. The Declaration of Independence asserted that all people were equal, and fashions began to follow suit. Gone were the days

*The Declaration of Independence promoted equality, so the wearing of wigs started to be viewed as pretentious.*

## Modern Wig Alternatives

People don't wear wigs as often today because there are many more alternatives to styling hair than in colonial times. Today, people with straight hair can get a permanent wave, and people with naturally curly hair can get their hair straightened. Hair can also be safely dyed almost any color imaginable.

To get more hair, people can use artificial hair integration—more commonly known as hair extensions or a weave. Using different techniques, human or artificial hair can be temporarily attached to a person's own hair. Anyone can get a long, luxurious style. People (usually men with male-pattern baldness) can even resort to surgery, having hair transplanted from one part of the head to another.

of ostentation, where a rich man would dress very differently than a poor man. Though there would always be income inequality, some of the obvious outward signs of difference began to lessen. Wigs, long a symbol of wealth and superiority, fell out of favor.

## The New Fashion

As is often the case, younger people set the fashion. Wigs became a hallmark of the older generation. Young men often paid just as much attention to their natural hair, though. Wigmakers began to focus more on their barbering and hairstyling skills. Now, they trimmed and curled more real hair than wigs.

France was always a leader in fashion, and at the time of the French Revolution that country was also at the forefront of ideas about liberty and equality. King Louis XVI was executed in 1793, the aristocracy was crushed, and it was a bad time to be a rich member of the nobility. Lots of wig-wearers ended up facing the guillotine.

By the 1800s, only elderly and very conservative men were wearing wigs. Some might still wear modest toupees—small patches of hair designed to conceal bald spots—but these weren't meant to be noticed the way wigs were. Women still used false curls and falls to supplement their hair, but the wigmaker's golden years had come to an end.

## Wigs Today

Of course, wigs are still in use today. In the United Kingdom, the kind of lawyer called a barrister usually has to wear a wig when he or she appears in court. They usually wear a short wig made out of horsehair, with curls at the side. Judges are often required to wear a wig, too. Sometimes they wear a short bench wig. For important or ceremonial occasions, though, they wear a long wig. Some people object to the wigs, and there have been several reforms to abolish the wigs in certain cases, or to make them optional.

## Entertainment and Style

One of the most common uses for wigs today is in the entertainment industry. Actors on stage, in operas, on television, and in the movies wear wigs either to improve their looks or to impersonate

someone else. The Metropolitan Opera, for example, has a chief wigmaker and a staff of six assistant wigmakers. They might make five hundred new wigs in a typical opera season, and maintain more than three thousand old wigs. The technique is still largely the same as it was in colonial times—carefully measure the head, and then weave the hairs in single strands or small batches. A human hair wig can take thirty to forty hours to make.

Everyday people wear wigs, too. Today, most wigs are purchased by women. Some choose to wear a wig because they have suffered hair loss. Certain diseases, and some medical treatments, such as chemotherapy, can cause hair to fall out. Other people view wigs as an easy way to have the style they want. Some people keep their hair short to make wig wearing easier. Others wear wig caps to keep their real hair smooth and hidden under the wig.

Wigs are no longer the symbols of status and wealth that they once were in colonial America. But for more than 150 years, the colonial wigmaker thrived. His wigs set the style for generations.

*Today, actors and singers, such as Lady Gaga, use wigs to change their looks. Most of them don't expect anyone to believe it is their real hair.*

# Glossary

apprentice
: A person bound to learn a trade from a master for a fixed period of years, usually for little or no pay.

aristocrat
: A member of the noble class; the elite.

barber
: A professional who cuts men's hair and generally also shaves or trims beards.

barber-surgeon
: A barber who also performed medical procedures; they were common on the battlefield or on ships.

blacksmith
: A person who uses tools such as a forge or anvil to craft and repair objects made of iron.

caul
: A close-fitting hair net; in wig-making, the cap that lies against the scalp, under the wig hair.

grizzle
: A color or pattern made up of a mixture of black and white.

henna
: Powder derived from a shrub that is used to color the hair and make temporary designs on the body.

journeyman
: The stage after apprenticeship but before becoming a master; a journeyman could be paid for his work.

master
: A skilled practitioner of a craft, one who has passed through apprentice and journeyman stages, and created a masterpiece.

periwig
: An old term for a wig, particularly a large, elaborate one; also peruke.

pomatum
: A pomade, or ointment used on the hair or scalp, that is often scented.

profit
: A financial gain made from work or investment.

Puritan
: A member of a sixteenth- and seventeenth-century Protestant group that demanded strict religious observation.

| smallpox | A very contagious disease marked by fever and skin pustules that often leave scars. |
| --- | --- |
| syphilis | A bacterial disease that begins as a sore and can progress to madness and death. |
| tempering | To improve the strength or elasticity of a substance, generally by heating and cooling. |
| widow | A woman whose husband has died. |
| wig | A false construction of hair worn for style or to conceal baldness. |

## Find Out More

### BOOKS

Heinrichs, Ann. *The Barber*. Colonial People. New York: Cavendish Square Publishing, 2010.

Krull, Kathleen. *Big Wig: A Little History of Hair*. New York: Scholastic, 2011.

Raum, Elizabeth. *The Dreadful, Smelly Colonies: The Disgusting Details About Life in Colonial America*. Minneapolis, MN: Capstone Press, 2011.

### WEBSITES

The History of the World of Hair

thehistoryofthehairsworld.com

This comprehensive website examines hairstyles and customs throughout history. Learn more about the Seleucid queen Berenice II of Egypt, Medusa, Samson, Rapunzel, and the Navajo People.

Random History: "Horrid Bushes of Vanity"—A History of Wigs

www.randomhistory.com/2009/02/24_wigs.html

From the earliest written records, both men and women have been fascinated by hair. This cornucopia of historical trivia has a section on the history of wigs.

Women and Children's Health Network: "A Hair Story"

www.cyh.com/HealthTopics/HealthTopicDetailsKids.aspx?p=335&id=2397&np=152

During the time of Elizabeth I of England, ladies used to pluck out some of their hair so that they looked like they had a very high forehead. Discover more stories about hair on this Kid's Health website.

## MUSEUM

Colonial Williamsburg

www.colonialwilliamsburg.com

This living history museum in Williamsburg, Virginia, recreates an entire colonial city. The 301-acre (102-hectare) site has many original historic buildings, and actor/docents who reenact colonial life. Explore stunning examples of American and British antiques and decorative art from the seventeenth, eighteenth, and nineteenth centuries.

# Index

Page numbers in **boldface** are illustrations. Entries in **boldface** are glossary terms.

## *About the Author*

Laura L. Sullivan is the author of many fiction and nonfiction books for children, including the fantasy *Under the Green Hill* and the romance *Love by the Morning Star*. She has also co-written an upcoming romantic mystery set in the Golden Age of Hollywood, with famed director and producer Adam Shankman. She is the author of many books for Cavendish Square, including six titles in the Colonial People series.